Woman With The Alabaster Jar

A Life Poured Out

MARY O. MOSS

Copyright © 2018 Mary O. Moss

All rights reserved.

ISBN: 1984163418
ISBN-13: 978-1984163417

DEDICATION

In loving memory of my mother,
Catherine D. Orth, who lives on in each of her five children, fifteen grandchildren, and three great grandchildren (each one her favorite). She left each person she met feeling valued and taught me that everyone has a story worth telling. Her party mix is legendary and she truly lived every day as if it was a great adventure.

And
Anne Houle, who lived with a tireless dedication to and pride in her family, especially her four grandchildren. She made hard things look easy, and good things even better with her infectious laughter. Hers was truly a life well-lived, that ended far too soon.

CONTENTS

Acknowledgments

Forward

Section 1 – The Valley of Dry Bones		6

Section 2 – The Years the Locust Has Eaten		21

Section 3 – The Alabaster Jar		39

ACKNOWLEDGMENTS

Many thanks to my friend, mentor and life coach, John-Erik Moseler, for his generosity of spirit and tireless guidance as he challenged me to just "do the thing." This book would not exist if not for his wisdom, encouragement, support and belief in my dreams.

I'm grateful to my husband, Jim Moss, who, during the creation of this book, was known to inquire on occasion, "did you work on the book today?" As in every area of my life, he is a source of strength and encouragement.

To my "Tribe." You are so special to me and I'm forever grateful for our connection, bond and friendship! Keep living into your dreams!

Thank you, to Jim Harris, artist, for his original painting, "Humble Adoration," for the book cover.

FOREWARD

Jesus left every person he touched, spoke to, even casually passed by, better off than before. Where there had been only brokenness, striving and suffering, he left them healed, grateful, hope-filled.

I had believed that every word of Jesus was spoken directly to me. "Do not let your hearts be troubled" (John 14:1 NLT). "So I say to you: Ask and it will be given to you; seek and you will find; knock and the door will be opened to you" (Luke 11:9 NIV). "Therefore I tell you, whatever you ask for in prayer, believe that you have received it, and it will be yours" (Mark 11:24 NIV). Such assurances!

But now my heart was troubled! Now I was not receiving what I had asked for! Now, I honestly couldn't even pray!

How then, do I reconcile that truth with my faith and mom's death? I did not feel his comforting hand on me—no healing power or command to weep no more! I was left incredulous that a faith so deep and studied and informed left me comfortless and alone.

God has been doing some hard work in me! My faith has become "on purpose" and "in spite of." When mom died, I realized my former faith was not enough to sustain me through the grief!

That is not/was not because of any lacking in God! Not at all! I see now that he was building me up in knowledge and endurance to prepare me to be at this place, right now. I needed a strong foundation and solid understanding of faith and grace and the Cross.

I'm not going to say my faith is comfortable exactly these days. It's not easier, either, and it's been hard-won. It's more settled though. Through these last few years I've been pretty deep in a pit and have been travelling out. Looking back on the journey, I see God's hand in every bit of it—in every minute of it! Hindsight so often gives us a perspective just not possible in the midst of an event or experience or journey.

I don't want my mom to be gone. But I am glad she's in heaven! How do I reconcile the two? I can't. I have to accept that she's gone and not be angry about it or I could never move on and out to a fuller and more meaningful life! I'm not angry! I am sad but, of course, that's tempered by the truth that she's in the presence of our great and glorious God. No more mental anguish. No more physical pain. No more struggling to make sense out of it all here on earth. Utter, indescribable, unimaginable peace: How could I deny her that?!

That is such solace! That, and the truth that I'll join her one day and our relationship will be beautiful and full of laughter and an ease that isn't always attainable in this realm. The love we have for each other will be manifested in ways I can't even fathom! I find myself caught some days between longing for that time and my desire to make the most of this time here on earth.

SECTION 1

THE VALLEY OF DRY BONES

THE VALLEY OF DRY BONES

"The hand of the Lord was on me, and he brought me out by the Spirit of the Lord and set me in the middle of a valley; it was full of bones. He led me back and forth among them, and I saw a great many bones on the floor of the valley, bones that were very dry. He asked me, "Son of man, can these bones live?"

I said, "Sovereign Lord, you alone know."

Then he said to me, "Prophesy to these bones and say to them, 'Dry bones, hear the word of the Lord! This is what the Sovereign Lord says to these bones: I will make breath enter you, and you will come to life. I will attach tendons to you and make flesh come upon you and cover you with skin; I will put breath in you, and you will come to life. Then you will know that I am the Lord.'"

So I prophesied as I was commanded. And as I was prophesying, there was a noise, a rattling sound, and the bones came together, bone to bone. I looked, and tendons and flesh appeared on them and skin covered them, but there was no breath in them.

Then he said to me, "Prophesy to the breath; prophesy, son of man, and say to it, 'This is what the Sovereign Lord says: Come, breath, from the four winds and breathe into these slain, that they may live.'" So I prophesied as he commanded me, and breath entered them; they came to life and stood up on their feet—a vast army.

Then he said to me: "Son of man, these bones are the people of Israel. They say, 'Our bones are dried up and our hope is gone; we are cut off.' Therefore prophesy and say to them: 'This is what the Sovereign Lord says: My people, I am going to open your graves and bring you up from them; I will bring you back to the land of Israel. Then you, my people, will know that I am the Lord, when I open your graves and bring you up from them. I will put my Spirit in you and you will live, and I will settle you in your own land. Then you will know that I the Lord have spoken, and I have done it, declares the Lord'" (Ezekiel 37:1-14 NIV).

Dry Bones of Our Lives

All around: hundreds, maybe thousands, of dry bones. All the dry bones of your past. The regrets. The things you did. The things you didn't do. The thoughts you had but never expressed. The thoughts you wish you had never expressed. The love you didn't give. The accolades you never received. The hurt you inflicted. The wounds of not being accepted or acknowledged. The pain you caused. The healing you didn't allow, the hurt that others inflicted upon you. The grief you never let go of.

A skull.
  Then a femur.
    Next a skeleton.
      Then another and another and another.
        As far and as wide as you can see...a valley full of dry bones.

And one morning you wake up feeling smothered—buried under this mile high, acres-wide desert of dry, wind-blown, whitewashed, stripped down bones.

Every dry bone from your life, stopping you from moving forward; attempting to keep you down. Whispering to you to stay put, rest awhile, linger for a day, a month, a year, a decade or more. The only way out is through. The only way through is to cast them aside to clear a path. Every one you kick aside shatters to a million pieces, gone forever! But never forgotten. How can you? The field is so vast, surely remnants of each memory will remain burned into your brain and tattooed on your heart forever.

God alone can restore us! God alone can redeem the past dry bones of our lives. He demands our faith – often when we have little left to lean on! But if we can hope, one more time; if we can trust, in this one last promise, He will do it! He will create out of our dry bones an army of love, and hope and faith, and rebuild our psyche and our lives to look and act and feel the way He sees us and designed us to be!

God is ready to breathe His spirit in us so that we may live, and live victoriously, in Him!

Hope and Grief

Hope and grief, so intertwined;
like a codependent dance with faltering steps.
1 and 2 and . . . 1 and 2 and . . .
1 and . . .

Grief takes no count of our present burden.
Hope sustains us through the long hours.
"I'm always here," hope declares.
"Be realistic," chimes in grief.
"I'm always here," hope whispers in reply.

Hope and grief, so enmeshed.
Like a braided cord unraveling thread by thread.
Taut from hanging on so long.
Grief so heavy, hope so light.
Force and counterforce, force and counterforce.

Grief and hope, an unrelenting journey
from light to dark and back again
A call, a look, a heart's desire; the crushing, endless wait
1 and 2 and . . . 1 and 2 and . . .
1 and . . .

Hope springs eternal through the dark night.
Grief awakens like a frightened child.
"I'm always here," hope reassures.
"I'm afraid," bemoans grief.
"I'm always here," hope whispers in reply.

A Passing Day

When mom died, I no longer had a certainty in my life. Yes, I grieved the loss of my parent, of her physical presence on earth. But, I guess what I equally grieved was <u>certainty</u> of life as I knew it; was that our nuclear family was no longer intact and whole. The family that had at its core: love, tradition, laughter, strength, intelligence, humor, astute thinking and passion for making the world a better place, helping.

Somehow all of that died for me too when she died. Perhaps I felt that way because I was largely alone in my grief as a majority of my nuclear family lived near each other, met together for celebrations and for remembrances—and I was a country away – on an opposite coast.

I didn't seek out a grief support group because I was "fine." Life went on, day in and day out, a world apart from where she had lived. All the "firsts" came and went after her death. And all the words within me died a gradual death. Life no longer was a grand adventure with well-charted vacation dates and destinations. Life became an outdated road atlas.

I recall a time I had gone to visit my college roommate's family. They lived a couple of hours away and we had never driven there by ourselves. Of course, she had no trouble navigating every turn, announcing every upcoming rest area, and scenic overlook, right up to the color of the mailboxes on her street on the way home. We headed back to school full of home cooking and happy memories.

As we got closer to town we weren't certain which turns to make! Overpass or underpass? Go South or East? We stopped at a gas station to ask for directions and they weren't sure where our street in the nearby college town exactly was. And they made a comment in passing that they had never taken the "new road" into town. We ultimately got their "old road" directions and found our way back.

I distinctly remember us making fun of them! "New road! Ha!" (They had meant the highway we had just exited from! It was at least 10 years old!)

Forty years later I completely understand their lack of need to ever use the new road! The old ones had stood them in good stead throughout their lifetimes—flooded out, snowed in, tree across the road causing a need for a detour—they had always been able to get where they needed to be—where they wanted to be – back at Ground Zero when that still meant the perfect place to be and it referred to the center of one's personal universe—and never even think about travelling on that new road.

When mom died, I found myself on that "new road" and it was *not* a place I had ever imagined, let alone thought about navigating! This story has come to mind periodically over the years for no particular reason and in no particular context! I think it might be like what Philip Yancey talks about: God gives us words (memories) that we don't necessarily understand in the perception of "a person trapped in time . . . not until history has run its course will we understand how all things work together for good."

Time has a different meaning for us than it does for God! His is an eternal, eons-and-eons perspective. Ours is one that only allows us to perceive years, months, days! I'm kind of in awe that a seemingly meaningless, random experience from so long ago, would serve me now, in the telling of this story. Not only that, he "nudged" my conscious memory of it over the years, as if to ensure I held it close for such a time as this. His timing is perfect.

"For you, a thousand years are as a passing day, as brief as a few night hours" (Psalm 90:4 NLT).

Knowing Full Well The Cost

There are places I just don't want to go.
Past hurts and dashed hopes and disappointments
I just have no desire to revisit them and yet . . .
I've held them close to me, clinging to them
Safe inside the wall of "life goes on."

God says, "Write your story," knowing full well the cost.
Past hurts and dashed hopes and disappointments.
They wrestle each other for my review and primary focus.
I've pushed them down and kept them at bay for so long!
Locked in the dark room of memory that reveals, "all is not as it seems."

Clenched fists, I rail at Him! "I do not want to tell this story!"
Past hurts and dashed hopes and disappointments.
A life poured out is just too close to the truth of it all.
I've lived these years as if in a constant dream state.
But the dream didn't really end even when I woke up.

I hesitate and hedge my bet and use every excuse I know.
Past hurts and dashed hopes and disappointments.
They weigh me down and hold me back, stifling that still small voice.
But still it finds its way clear of all the noise and confusion.
I just don't have the courage to breathe new life into pain.

God stands firm in his determination and plan.
Past hurts and dashed hopes and disappointments.
He lifts them all to Him and binds up every one.
They lose their power when He sanctifies the pain.
God says, "write your story," so the future can be redeemed.

God says, "Write your story," knowing full well the cost.

No Shortcut Through The Grief

There is no shortcut through the grief.

The interment for my mom was on a Friday, a few weeks after the funeral, and I wasn't there. I didn't think I would mind initially, but I did. I know it's "just a ceremony" but I would have liked to be there for a final "goodbye" with my dad, sisters and brother. It was just so far to travel, and I had used most of my paid time off by extending my visit after she died.

My dad and I drove out to the site while I was still in Seattle. It poured rain all the way out there -- just a gray, cold, morning. As we pulled into the cemetery the sky cleared and the rain stopped! By the time we headed back to the house it was a bright sunny day! I think it was Mom's way of letting me know she and I had our own personal goodbye that day.

It was hard to leave Seattle for home that first time after the funeral service - harder than ever before, because I knew it would never be the same going back. Hard because I knew there would be no more birthday cards, anniversary cards, no more Party Mix packed in Christmas boxes, all "mom-hallmarks."

There are some pretty hard moments in the early days—when it still didn't seem real! As a way of celebrating mom's life when we returned home after the funeral, my daughter baked a batch of ginger cookies using the recipe we included in Mom's obituary. My son and I had several conversations about Mom and some of the funny things she did and said - and the little things that made her special. We even speculated about future elections and what Mom/Grandma would think and who she would support (from a great vantage point)! All the things we loved about her will live on and her legacy will continue. But it was tough when it was still so new--too hard to wrap our heads around.

It took a long time to be at the point that I don't cry every time I remember she's gone. Somehow life goes on. Go to work. Fix dinner. Go to bed. Get up again and do it all again. I know that sounds trite.

It's how we go on, though. And going on is really the only option. It's how we get through each day.

It's so hard in those early days. It requires sheer force of will just to turn over and get out of bed in the morning. It involves striving not to curl up in a little ball and cry like a baby. When the truth that she's gone is still fresh, it stays in the back of our minds during every conversation and through every activity. In the moments when we allow the sadness, loss and pain to creep in, it can be almost unbearable all over again.

Over the years it has gotten better. I know there will always be "moments." And there will always be reason to smile at her memory and celebrate her life.

"He will wipe every tear from their eyes. There will be no more death or mourning or crying or pain, for the old order of things has passed away" (Revelation 21:4 NIV).

When All The Earth Has Passed Away

Do not grieve for your past sorrow
Do not remain in today
Do not rely upon tomorrow
Because the earth will one day pass away

When all the earth has passed away
When no more songs are left to sing
When no more words are still to say
When death has lost its piercing sting

Do not grieve for your past sorrow
Do not remain in today
Do not rely upon tomorrow
Because the earth will one day pass away

When time stands still and heaven alone remains
When I kneel before His glorious throne
And God declares His shining glory still reigns
Heaven will become my forever home

Do not grieve for your past sorrow
Do not remain in today
Do no rely upon tomorrow
Because the earth will one day pass away

SECTION 2

THE YEARS THE LOCUST HAS EATEN

The Years the Locust Has Eaten

25 "So I will restore to you the years that the swarming locust has eaten,
The crawling locust,
The consuming locust,
And the chewing locust,[a]
My great army which I sent among you.
26 You shall eat in plenty and be satisfied,
And praise the name of the LORD your God,
Who has dealt wondrously with you;
And My people shall never be put to shame.
27 Then you shall know that I *am* in the midst of Israel:
I *am* the LORD your God
And there is no other.
My people shall never be put to shame.

God's Spirit Poured Out
28 "And it shall come to pass afterward
That I will pour out My Spirit on all flesh;
Your sons and your daughters shall prophesy,
Your old men shall dream dreams,
Your young men shall see visions.
29 And also on My menservants and on My maidservants
I will pour out My Spirit in those days.
30 "And I will show wonders in the heavens and in the earth:
Blood and fire and pillars of smoke.
31 The sun shall be turned into darkness,
And the moon into blood,
Before the coming of the great and awesome day of the Lord.
32 And it shall come to pass
That whoever calls on the name of the Lord
Shall be [b]saved.
For in Mount Zion and in Jerusalem there shall be [c]deliverance,
As the Lord has said,
Among the remnant whom the Lord calls.

Joel 2:25-32 (NKJV)

The Broken, Scarred, Wounded and Damaged

I'm the farthest thing from perfect anyone can imagine! I've fought demons and I still fight them—will probably fight them 'til the end of my days, but they're not as prevalent—and not as strong now as they have been. And I guess they're actually serving as the thorn in my side that will keep me humble! I do very clearly and succinctly recall exactly from whence I came!

Kind of crazy, but my writer's brain, which has long since been on "mute" since mom died has started overtaking my thoughts! It's as disconcerting as it is exciting! The more I "exercise" those muscles, the more it happens!

Oh, my goodness, but God is good! I had strayed so far away from His comfort, guidance, direction and desire for my life—and now to be wooed back to His tender care and comfort is unbelievable. He's empowering me and inspiring me to become an even better version of myself—to write better, to be more authentic and transparent—and I'm not afraid now! It's still hard, but He is helping me be brave. I exchanged emails recently with a dear friend and the closing sentence to the last one I sent her: "Look at me, a hot mess, all full of wisdom for others!"

Those years I spent in the wilderness of my grief were necessary. They shaped me and refined me and helped mold me to more closely resemble God's vision of me. I needed to have everything that was not of Him, for Him, by Him, worn away, burned off and discarded. Then He worked with the skeletal remains to rebuild me into His vision. I doubted I would ever say again, "Such a loving, gracious God even after my roaming far from Him; not heeding His call; rejecting His wisdom; refusing His will." It's sinful! But I know it was necessary, so I could arrive at this point; necessary so I could speak the truth in love and through His power.

Do not believe you are too far gone for God to reclaim you! He does His best work with the broken, the scarred, the wounded and the damaged. He takes even those who have run from him, denied him, refused him and re-purposes it all to create a masterpiece! We are masterpieces, just waiting to take shape. Do not be discouraged or afraid! He can do amazing things out of our ravages. I promise you, He can redeem and restore you if you'll surrender to His power and love! I'm living proof. Out of our grief, he creates new life.

"He heals the brokenhearted And binds up their wounds"(Psalm 147:3 NASB).

Baptized By The Future

A blur
Mindless wandering
      Desperate searching
           Gripping despair
                Crushing shame
                      Wounded soul
                          Broken heart
                              Shattered psyche

Start from scratch
In love with a dream
      A life's cause rediscovered
           Breathed back to Life
                Strengthened by hope
                      Fueled by faith
                          Washed clean by grace
                              Baptized by the future

A dying ember turned bonfire
A mess becomes a message
      The pain becomes a cure
           Determination
                Purpose
                      Progress
                          Mountaintop
                              Gratitude

The Lord restores the years the locust has eaten.

An Appointed Time

There is an appointed time for everything. And there is a time for every [a]event under heaven—
² A time to give birth and a time to die;
A time to plant and a time to uproot what is planted.
³ A time to kill and a time to heal;
A time to tear down and a time to build up.
⁴ A time to weep and a time to laugh;
A time to mourn and a time to dance.
⁵ A time to throw stones and a time to gather stones;
A time to embrace and a time to shun embracing.
⁶ A time to search and a time to give up as lost;
A time to keep and a time to throw away.
⁷ A time to tear apart and a time to sew together;
A time to be silent and a time to speak.
⁸ A time to love and a time to hate;
A time for war and a time for peace.
⁹ What profit is there to the worker from that in which he toils?
¹⁰ I have seen the task which God has given the sons of men with which to occupy themselves.
¹¹He has made everything [b]appropriate in its time. He has also set eternity in their heart, [c]yet so that man will not find out the work which God has done from the beginning even to the end.
(Ecclesiastes 3:1-11 NASB)

I used to love the cadence of these verses. I was captivated by the beauty of the rhythm and the words had a way of almost rocking me into a sense of calm at the assurance that all life – all creation – was designed with a purpose, and for a reason, and that the time and place of birth and death – the full circle of life – was pre-destined with love and intent.

I had clung to the hope that the "season and time" for my mom's life on this earth was not waning. I had a subtle confidence that approached outright denial that she would succumb to the aggressive cancer she fought against for close to a year.

These words rang hollow for me after she died. I look back and think of life before and after like living in a room with a veil down the middle. A trip to the ER might move us closer to the veil, a hospitalization closer still. But a prognosis of X number of months to live? That puts one just the other side of the divide. Still observing life in this realm, it all must move as slow motion, slower and slower as the time approaches.

Through the lens of 80 years or 90, or more, a day seems like a small price to pay for the luxury of idleness and procrastination. A month, year, decade, seems a short time to hold on to resentment, anger, envy, hate, fear. Moving to just the other side of the veil, surely every event, every word, and thought must race through the mind and illicit every emotion imaginable!

Does life flash before one's eyes in that final moment? For my mom I believe it unfolded, decade by decade, year by year, month by month, day by day, hour by hour. And as the end approached, I hope she breathed a deep sigh of both gratitude and awe! She left a legacy that she surely never imagined nor conceived possible in her mid-West, farm-girl practicality-structured imagination!

My faith is not nearly as simple these days as it once was! It's no longer soft and airy, light and almost breathless! It's tougher and "sturdier." It's a more practical and realistic faith. But it's becoming a deep and abiding faith! I couldn't say that for a long time. For a long time, I don't think I had any faith at all. I've been dipping my toes back into the Bible. I've been revisiting prayer and even started attending church again sometimes. I've been reading devotions and going back through past writings proclaiming my earlier faith.

And I'm settling in. My faith is genuine and real these days. I'm choosing to have faith, "in spite of." I fully accept and acknowledge that I, and everyone in my world, will one day die. When you know that – with a true knowing and acceptance – it changes your perception of what God's timing looks like.

"For you, a thousand years are as a passing day, as brief as a few night hours" (Psalm 90:4 NLT).

When we get past the trial; when we pass through the desert; when we see the Promised Land again, we enter with a deeper, stronger, "on purpose" faith! God does, indeed, provide for us. We are divinely designed and planned for his purpose in his time and by his design. Considering he chose us, it seems to me only fitting that I not only repent, but, rejoice that He loved me even before I turned away. He wooed me in my self-imposed isolation from His care. He rejoices that I am finding my way back!

"... But while he was still a long way off, his father saw him [his prodigal son] and was filled with compassion for him; he ran to his son, threw his arms around him and kissed him. The son said to him, 'Father, I have sinned against heaven and against you. I am no longer worthy to be called your son.' But the father said to his servants, 'Quick! Bring the best robe and put it on him. Put a ring on his finger and sandals on his feet. Bring the fattened calf and kill it. Let's have a feast and celebrate. For this son of mine was dead and is alive again; he was lost and is found.' So they began to celebrate" (Luke 15:20-24 NIV)

Faithful and True

Hibernation

Alienation

Consternation

and

Rumination

Give way to

Eagerness

Reconciliation

Amazement

and

Anticipation

As

remnants of winter still grapple for a foothold

and spring stops, starts and bounds forth.

"And He who sits on the throne said, "Behold, I am making all things new ." And He said, "Write, for these words are faithful and true"" (Revelation 21:5 NASB).

Petunias

On a Wednesday night, not too long after mom died, I dreamt/saw in my mind (I was half awake I think, but not sure) Mom standing in her driveway. That hallmark little smile on her face. Right arm bent, shoulder strap on her shoulder, purse resting in the crook of her arm, ready to go off to whatever adventure the day held.

I had had an unsettled feeling all day and had trouble sleeping. Throughout the night, after this vision, I continued trying to glean what message she was sending me. Ultimately, I realized she had come through the spirit world to say good bye.

The next evening, I had to chuckle at myself as I went to the mailbox and noticed my petunias around the mailbox had not been "deadheaded" in quite some time. Mom always did that for me when she was at my house - and she was meticulous about that in her own yard. So, I picked off all the dried up, dead heads and smiled. I'm pretty sure she wanted to let me know "you've got this;" and, "you always did;" which she had told me once years ago. But I didn't feel like I did! Still I want her here. I think she stopped off for a final parting. But I wasn't ready to let her go. . .

"Blessed are the poor in spirit, for theirs is the kingdom of heaven. Blessed are those who mourn, for they will be comforted. Blessed are the meek, for they shall inherit the earth" (Matthew 5:3-5 NIV).

I'm Still Here

I'm still here.
I'm in the wind.
I'm in the twinkling stars.
I'm in the shadows of the moon.

I'm still here.
I'm in each breath and every sigh.
I'm in a random sideways glance.
I'm in your laughter and fun.

I'm still here.
I'm in the snowflakes and rain.
I'm in rainbows and sunshine.
I'm in clouds and clear skies.

I'm still here.
I'm in mountain heather.
I'm in the deep, deep sea.
I'm in craggy rocks and sea shells.

I'm still here.
I'm in all your teardrops.
I'm in each struggle you endure.
I'm in every victory and celebration.

I'm still here.
I am with you always because you are part of me.
You are my heart and love and
my everything and always will be.

I'm still here.
Live a long and happy life
Be kind and gentle.
Do what is right and good to honor me.

Don't worry . . . it's good . . . it's good

Comfort Abounds

Every once in a while, I catch a glimpse of two things. First is the person I really want to be - all the time - even in crunch time - even in times of stress - even when in pain - yes, even if I were to lay dying. It's who I saw my mother become in the last year of her life. The transformation was nothing short of a miracle; an example of God answering prayers in ways we can never imagine. Mom had a healing--not of her body, but of all her worries, burdens and pain. It was a healing I know we all pray for ourselves in the here and now and at the end of our lives. But I don't think any of us ever really thought about asking God to really, truly, absolutely and completely grant her the kind of peace on earth she - and we - experienced throughout her cancer journey (and our journey with her and my dad). It was nothing short of a miracle. And a gift - real gift that I will never be able to thank God for enough.

I want to be that person now. I want to be whole and happy and at peace and to feel - and live as if I feel - blessed. Every day. All the time. Through pain. Through disappointment. Through everything. The second thing I glimpse sometimes (probably not often enough) is who I really am. And I wince when that person looks back at me in the mirror of my mind. I'm not a terrible person. But I've done so many things of which I am not proud. I've acted badly and been selfish, self-righteous and yes, just downright sinful. I'm not "that person" all the time. I just act like that person sometimes. And I don't like that person at all.

I am trying very hard these days to be more like the person I want to be--and desperately hope to become. Because I am so very blessed. So, so blessed. When I say I'm blessed it doesn't mean I have everything I ever wanted! (Though I certainly have far more than I deserve). Blessed is state of mind and heart. It has become my way of "being" (or at least my attempt to be this way).

God is so very good and I can't help but praise him for every blessing. My prayer today - and each and every day I am alive - is that I speak words of love and kindness. That I think thoughts only of others and how I can minister to them. That I think only thoughts of

God's grace and healing. And while I am certain I will never be the person I truly want to be; I learned through my mom's final months and in the months since, that God's will is infallible. He answers prayers we cannot even dare to utter. He hears our cries for hope and help and healing that are uttered in soundless, breathless sobs. And He answers. So, I pray.

I really miss my mom a lot some days. It sneaks up on me. It hits me out of the blue. And then I remember that she told us she was happier than she had ever been in her life weeks before she died. Blessed is, I think, what she meant. For perhaps the first time she was able to see her life from an eternal view point. One that surpasses all human toiling, striving, struggling and dreaming. Perhaps she realized she had everything she could ever have hoped for - and far more than she deserved - more than any of us deserve.

I want to live like that every day. I want it to seep into my heart and my mind and into every cell of my body. I want to live blessed - not like I'm blessed - live rightly because I *am* blessed. My mom taught me many things throughout my life and touched many people throughout hers. Being blessed is perhaps the most significant lesson of all. And she was. And I was, and always will be, as her daughter.

"Praise be to the God and Father of our Lord Jesus Christ, the Father of compassion and the God of all comfort, who comforts us in all our troubles, so that we can comfort those in any trouble with the comfort we ourselves receive from God. For just as we share abundantly in the sufferings of Christ so also our comfort abounds through Christ" (2 Corinthians 1:3-5 NIV).

SECTION 3

THE ALABASTER JAR

Woman With The Alabaster Jar

³⁶ When one of the Pharisees invited Jesus to have dinner with him, he went to the Pharisee's house and reclined at the table. ³⁷ A woman in that town who lived a sinful life learned that Jesus was eating at the Pharisee's house, so she came there with an alabaster jar of perfume. ³⁸ As she stood behind him at his feet weeping, she began to wet his feet with her tears. Then she wiped them with her hair, kissed them and poured perfume on them.

³⁹ When the Pharisee who had invited him saw this, he said to himself, "If this man were a prophet, he would know who is touching him and what kind of woman she is—that she is a sinner."

⁴⁰ Jesus answered him, "Simon, I have something to tell you."
"Tell me, teacher," he said.

⁴¹ "Two people owed money to a certain moneylender. One owed him five hundred denarii,[a] and the other fifty. ⁴² Neither of them had the money to pay him back, so he forgave the debts of both. Now which of them will love him more?"

⁴³ Simon replied, "I suppose the one who had the bigger debt forgiven."
"You have judged correctly," Jesus said.

⁴⁴ Then he turned toward the woman and said to Simon, "Do you see this woman? I came into your house. You did not give me any water for my feet, but she wet my feet with her tears and wiped them with her hair. ⁴⁵ You did not give me a kiss, but this woman, from the time I entered, has not stopped kissing my feet. ⁴⁶ You did not put oil on my head, but she has poured perfume on my feet. ⁴⁷ Therefore, I tell you, her many sins have been forgiven—as her great love has shown. But whoever has been forgiven little loves little."
⁴⁸ Then Jesus said to her, "Your sins are forgiven."
⁴⁹ The other guests began to say among themselves, "Who is this who even forgives sins?"
⁵⁰ Jesus said to the woman, "Your faith has saved you; go in peace."

(Luke 7:36-50 NIV)

All Things New

Shame is not your name
Regret is not your mantra
Grief is not your home
Your past is not your destiny
Today is not the end
Doubt is not your friend
Fear is not your reality

Redeemed is your new identity
Hope is your new lifesong
Joy is your new dwelling place
Grace is your new existence
Tomorrow is a new beginning
Belief is your new companion
Courage is your new truth

"Therefore if anyone is in Christ, a new creation has come; the old is gone, the new is here!" (2 Corinthians 5:17 NIV).

The Club Nobody Wants to Join

Grief is a club with open membership, but nobody wants to join! Whether we grieve over the death of a loved one, the end of a marriage or long-term relationship, loss of a job, even when a pet dies, grief, like birth and death, is a universal experience.

God does his best work in us, often, in spite of us! Today there were tears! They had been lurking just under the surface; waiting to well up in me! I thought I had gone deep enough, explored widely and thoroughly enough to bypass more tears. But they are necessary for me to heal! The tears have been holding back, patiently waiting to do their job. I have stuffed them down and pushed back every time I felt them surfacing over the past few years. They are necessary to travel to the other side of grief where there is healing, hope and even joy. Those are only possible when we allow grief to do its work.

I do not want the tears to fall, but I now have no choice! They fall, unbidden, unwanted, bitterly and hesitantly—releasing so much more than the grief of one loss or two. There is a release of all sense of control and power and certainty, pride, scorn, regret! How can such powerlessness lead to healing and wholeness? It happens when we surrender everything we think we know, believe, understand, and everything we are or have been. The great heaving sobs of a life poured out inform me that while I am greatly loved and deeply desired by a God I cannot even fathom . . . I am small and powerless without Him and His love, His direction.

Grief is a universal language and there is no shortcut through it! In fact I'm certain that because I refused to walk with it and in it when mom died, and recently when a dear friend died, the work is harder, cuts deeper and hurts more, and is now mixed with regret and dismay that I was so stubborn.

Perhaps grief's role in God's magnificent design is 2-fold: to draw us ever closer to Him and to ensure that moving forward, we cherish moments, experiences, celebrations and triumphs fully and wholeheartedly. If that is "all we get" in life we are blessed!

Even though years may pass, and in spite of full and fruitful lives, grief remains a constant companion. It is important not to be consumed by it, to not stay stuck there. Perhaps grief serves as a reminder to cherish those still with us; to forgive a little more freely; to work a little harder to understand one another; to strive always for gentleness and grace when others hurt us or disappoint us.

Grief becomes transformative when it guides us to let go of a personal agenda, to loosen our grasp on our plans for our lives; to seek a higher purpose and ultimately claim our identity—not as a son or daughter, spouse, parent, lover, friend, companion or acquaintance – but as God's.

We remain trapped in that Nethersphere between life and death forever, unless we allow grief to do its work; to guide us to a new way of being. When we surrender "me" to the power of "Him," we begin the process of becoming whole again.

The journey through grief is dark and lonely, bitter and even surreal. We don't deal well with change—particularly a change that rocks our world! The only way through it is through it. Amid our grief, it is unimaginable that God would ask us to relinquish anything else to Him and yet he does. He requires that we relinquish our question, "Why?"

"Oh, the depth of the riches and wisdom and knowledge of God! How unsearchable his judgments, and his path beyond tracing out! "Who has known the mind of the Lord, or who has been his counselor?" Who has ever given to God, that God should repay them?" (Romans 11:33-35 NIV)

Dichotomy

I say I do not need the approval of others
Yet I seek it constantly
I think I do not need permission to speak my mind
Yet I hold back all too often
I say I do not need the wisdom of sages
Yet I long for it continually
I think I do not need comfort and ease
Yet I pray for both daily
I say I do not need friendship
Yet I ache with loneliness
I think I do not need a heart for God
Yet I fail in my humanity continually
I say I can make the journey alone
Yet I fall before I even begin

Today, I reconsider

Grief Is Not The End

We don't grieve only for the new emptiness in our lives. We grieve also for the loss of "one more chance" to love well, to express gratitude, to forgive. It's just a complicated mess! But grief is not the end. Our loss also, though, offers us the opportunity to channel our energy and force of our grief to create something life-giving and remarkable, "in memory of" and "in honor of." Perhaps that is how we fill the emptiness that remains. Nothing is wasted in God's economy!

I wonder what the world would be like if we lobbied for or against causes while our loved ones were still living—what if we didn't fill our lives so full of activities and striving for things that are not eternal, but rather recognized something to honor each other and commit to share that with the world now—today! What if we take up causes beyond the significance only in the here and now, only for the fleeting span of our life time on earth: trophies, money, power, fame, striving, chasing. What if we took a breath and leaned in to what we too often tragically wait for grief to inform: life is short! One day there will not be another chance. All too soon we'll look back and mourn all the what ifs and if onlies, even before the grieving takes hold.

That is the only way I can make sense of grief! I don't like it—despise it and all that it is! But if I am to accept the reality of it, I must believe it serves a purpose in our lives, just like love and joy and awe and every good thing we know of this life.

If I divide my faith life as I do my life, mom's death is the axis of before and after. A new dynamic is being established. There is a now and a "future now." That is where hope and healing reside! Life throws us for a loop sometimes and we experience, "mini deaths" along our journey. Our dreams are stalled, or completely derailed. A marriage ends. Our career is taken from us. Our plans and hopes and our certainty all fall away. It's odd that even though we experience these lesser losses, we are ill-prepared for the big loss of death. Practice does not always make perfect!

In spite of my previously active, well-informed and joyfully practiced faith, God did not let me have my way to keep my mom with us! So, then the discussion goes to faith! Does it only sustain me when everything is going my way? Do I have faith only in the hope of answered prayers and problems solved? Do I still believe—even from the pit of my grief—that God is *for me*?

I'm not angry at God. I don't think I ever was. I certainly was disappointed though! And then I just cut Him off, deciding there was no way I would "win" this one, because my prayers had unquestionably gone unanswered. I felt ignored and unloved, unimportant, unworthy, undeserving and abandoned.

In hindsight, with reflection and prayer, I realize each lesser death is intended to draw us closer to God. Each loss of earthly gain is to be channeled into a God-sized win that only heaven can provide. While we feel alone on our journey through grief, it's important to remember that God understands our mourning, and He walks through ours with us. The truth of the risen Christ gives us hope that in a while our sadness will turn to rejoicing. The resurrection reminds us that one day we too will be born into a new heaven and a new earth! Eventually, we learn to sing again – and rejoice that heaven awaits us all. And that is indeed cause to sing and clap our hands.

"Clap your hands, all you nations; shout to God with cries of joy" (Psalm 47:1 NIV).

One Most Ardent, Unanswered Prayer

My one most ardent, unanswered prayer.
Made me believe God didn't even care.
When my mother died, all my dreams became tainted.
My faith faltered, grew shaky and finally fainted.

I was living in faith and believing His word.
His great promises were the sweetest thing I'd ever heard.
So many prayers He had granted in the past.
But that one most ardent, unanswered prayer left me aghast.

I forgot where I came from and to whom I belonged.
That one most ardent, unanswered prayer made me feel wronged.
I turned away from saints, angels and the Cross.
I shut down the pain and disappointment of my great loss.

My journey was on purpose and for a purpose in God's great plan.
I didn't think my life could go on, but God showed me that it can.
That one most ardent, unanswered prayer brought me here.
Now my life has renewed purpose and I'm living on a new higher tier.

My desert time brought me to this current oasis.
I'm no longer living as if my mom's loss was an unredeemable crisis.
My mess has become a message and my test a testimony.
My grief and pain no longer carry the sting of acrimony.

My one most ardent, unanswered prayer makes me more like Christ.
Though I can never repay him, I love him deeply for what he sacrificed.
He knows about disappointment and pain just like me and you.
His one most ardent prayer was unanswered too.

And it changed the world.

Chicken Heart

One of my friends told me years ago she thought I was so brave! I was a little surprised by that characterization! I had never even thought about myself in that light. As I view my life and my mother's life through a different filtered lens since Mom's death, I now realize that perhaps what my friend saw in me was really a grand sense of adventure! Everything my mom did was an adventure -- whether it was going to the grocery store, the mall or library, eating dinner out or enjoying visits to Mexico, Hawaii or Europe!

My daughter shared an observation/memory about my mother "bouncing around town with an easy-going smile and more energy than seemed natural for a woman of her years." Up until the very end of her life, she had that bounce, and even at the end, that easy-going smile! I've intentionally focused on having an "easy-going" smile recently. And I have noticed almost everyone smiles back - even stressed, self-involved drivers in parking lots, at stop lights and people I pass by at the grocery store. And I find my own spirits lifted when I remember to smile.

You know, as I think about it, Mom instilled that sense of adventure in all of us - at least in subtle ways. Years ago, our family went on one of our annual family vacations to Nag's Head, NC. It rained and rained and rained. Picture this: 2 adults 5 children, the beach, rain, rain, rain. So, what did Mom do? She taught us all to play a Midwestern card game, Euchre. (It's kind of like poker, bridge, spades.) Since that year - and we were young - when four or five of us are together a Euchre game ensues. If one needed to leave for work or some other commitment, somebody would slide in and take their place. All of the 15 grandchildren learned to play Euchre as soon as they were old enough to sit still. It was just a given in our family -- you learned to play Euchre – and so did friends, boyfriends, girlfriends, spouses, grandchildren!

Sometimes when everyone is together -- two tables are going, along with a Risk game - with an assortment of cousins, friends, either playing or sitting around providing color commentary. When I was in Seattle after my mom's death, one of my nephews told a story that so perfectly captures Mom! (Several of us were, of course, playing Euchre as he shared his story!) He and a cousin were playing against Grandma and another cousin. He was hesitating, uncertain as to whether he should declare trump. He said, "Grandma told me "Don't be a chicken heart!"" (Not mean at all, but rather, in her very matter-of-fact way.) Ultimately, Grandma's team trounced him and his partner! She consoled him by telling him "It's okay! At least you went for it."

Mom was definitely not a chicken heart! And I thank God I inherited that from her! I've done a lot of things people didn't think I could do (especially myself!). I've self-published books, started businesses, took on creative projects and undertaken everything in my life with "all-in" determination, and -- I now realize -- approached everything I've ever done with that sense of "even if things didn't turn out as I wanted/expected, at least I could look back and say I tried." Yes. I'd say I am my mother's daughter!

"Therefore, since we have such a hope, we are very bold"
(2 Corinthians 3:12 NIV).

WOMAN WITH THE ALABASTER JAR

Where I Am From

I am from newspaper women
and farmer's wives
spines of steel
wisdom beyond imagining
no dreams of fame and fortune
just ordinary lives

I am from hard work and ancient wounds
never forgotten nor spoken of
nor exposed to light of day
survival of the fittest
overcoming struggle
manifesting deep love

I am from the ocean and the sand
eternal horizon expanding
waves crash and roar
undertow pulls and releases
shells and skeletons from the deep
a million grains of understanding

I am from ancient earth mothers
sisters of magic and mystery
creators of hope and beauty
vessels of future dreams
dutifully bearing children
changing the course of history

I am from spirit and flesh and bone
made to wonder "why?"
seeking ever after truth
needing only the next question
asking always for the answer
looking ever to God in the sky

I am from the earth and sky
thriving where nothing should grow

dirt and clouds, sun and rain
blooming where I'm planted
desiring only air and water
sometimes reaping more than I sow

I am from woman and man
destiny, desire and chance
created in an image and likeness
struggling to be different
resigned to be who I am
rising above my circumstance

I am from saints and angels
wings of gossamer and gold
seen from the corner of my eye
whispers and quiet breezes
in my head and on my skin
heavenly secrets in dreams unfold

I am from the eternal source of life
created for a purpose and a reason
perfectly and divinely designed
journeying toward heaven
offering up my future and my past
each twist and turn in time and season

Mysterious and Magnificent

Throughout the months of mom's cancer, and certainly since her death, there have been spells of anger, fear, sadness, and grief at the anticipated/probable loss we were told was coming. Of course, death is inevitable, and Mom was 81 years old. But I wasn't ready. Can one ever be?

Mom's body was dead but her spirit, her joining of the eternal, infinite life force that I believe is God was stunningly magical, mysterious and, yes, magnificent! We all felt her after she died at random times, in odd moments--certain that it could only have been her spirit! We are sure she frequently swooped back down to earth - not yet ready to leave us alone - knowing we still needed her.

That's so like Mom though - turning back from heaven to finish the care-taking we still craved - gently ushering us into the next stage of our own lives here on earth without her. We live in our bodies as a temporary state, housing our souls for a few decades, or more if we are fortunate. But what comes after is unspeakable! I know as the end approached Mom must have been anxious to get to heaven. Certainly, the existence that comes next is so marvelous, so spectacular, so transcendent of anything we can imagine that I know she was just blown away when she arrived in heaven!

In the ensuing years God has granted me a peace that has not yet begun to smooth out the rough edges of my grief, but that I trust and believe will sustain me until I join Mom in heaven.

Eternity might just be long enough for the woman who never met a stranger to find out where everyone there in heaven came from! I'm pretty sure the feasting and celebrating there has reached a crescendo that will last for centuries. I know without question that Jesus is the first person she saw and that she looped her arm around his, patted his hand told him, "Thank you honey, for hanging on the Cross for me. You didn't have to do that! I would have loved you anyway."

I am so blessed to have my family - husband, children, father, siblings, nieces and nephews, uncles, aunts and cousins - numbering in the hundreds. We are a force to be reckoned with in this life - and I can't wait to see what all of us, joining with those who await us now, can do.

I love you, Mom. I miss you. But it's good. . . it's good.

"Do not let your heart be troubled. You believe in God, believe also in Me. My Father's house has many rooms; if it were not so, would I have told you I go to prepare a place for you? And if I go and prepare a place for you, I will come again and take you with me, that you also may be where I am. You know the way to the place where I am going" (John 14:1-4 NIV).

WOMAN WIH THE ALABASTER JAR

ABOUT THE AUTHOR

Mary Moss is a poet, author and speaker. Her first book, "Woman At The Well," recounts her discovery of the many facets of God's grace in our lives! It is a liberating adventure that offers encouragement, sustenance and joy. Like this current work, it includes both original poems and short devotions. Both can be a great study for a book group as well as personal daily devotions.

Mary wears man hats! She has served as a Stephen Ministry Leader, a Certified Lay Speaker in the United Methodist Church, and has earned a certificate in Congregational Leadership through the Baptist Theological Seminary in Richmond, VA. She has taught courses in Frugal Living, Introduction to Journaling, Journaling and Prayer, Creative Writing, Becoming God's Wonder Woman, and others.

Writer, speaker, Biblical storyteller, columnist, retreat leader and occasional blogger, Mary is a prolific writer, a creative and energetic woman with a passion for life and a deep and abiding faith in Jesus. Mary is also a devoted wife, loving mother and doting grandmother, true blue friend, and child of God. Jobs? Mary has had just about any you can think of! "Jill of all trades" and master of some, she leans on the Lord to make it through every day—every hour. Okay . . . every minute. Oh! And coffee . . . lots of coffee!

To request Mary for a retreat or speaking engagement, visit her website:
Divinelydesigned.us

Connect with Mary on line at
fb.com/themarymoss
fb.com/themarymossauthor

NOTES/REFLECTIONS

NOTES/REFLECTIONS

NOTES/REFLECTIONS

NOTES/REFLECTIONS

Made in the USA
Middletown, DE
25 August 2018